How

Out Of Debt

In 50 Days

Dr. Bob Rodgers

HOW TO GET
OUT OF DEBT
IN 50 DAYS

Unless otherwise indicated, all scripture quotations are
taken from the King James Version of the Bible.

CHAPTER 1

How To Get Out Of Debt In 50 Days

"And when the day of Pentecost was fully come, they were all with one accord in one place and suddenly there came a sound from heaven as of a rushing mighty wind, and it filled the entire house where they were sitting. And there appeared unto them cloven tongues like as of fire, and it sat upon each of them. And they were all filled with the Holy Ghost, and began to speak with other tongues, as the Spirit gave them utterance. And there were dwelling at Jerusalem Jews, devout men, out of every nation under heaven. Now when this was noised abroad, the multitude came together, and was confounded, because that every man heard them speak in his own language. And they were all amazed and marveled, saying one to another, Behold, are not all these which speak Galileans? "And how hear we every man in our own tongue, wherein we were born? Parthians, and Medes, and Examines, and the dwellers in Mesopotamia, and in Judea, and Cappadocia, in Pontus, and Asia, Phrygia, and Pamphylia, in Egypt, and in the parts of Libya about Cyrene, and strangers of Rome, Jews and proselytes, "Cretes and Arabians, we do hear them speak in our tongues the wonderful works of God 'And they were all amazed, and were in doubt saying one to another, What meaneth this?' Others mocking said, these men are full of new wine. "But Peter, standing up with the

eleven, lifted up his voice, and said unto them, Ye men of Judea, and all ye that dwell at Jerusalem, be this known unto you, and hearken to my words: For these are not drunken, as ye suppose, seeing it is but the third hour of the day. But this is that which was spoken by the prophet Joel; "And it shall come to pass in the last days, saith God, I will pour out of my Spirit upon all flesh: and your sons and your daughters shall prophesy, and your young men shall see visions, and your old men shall dream dreams:" Acts 2:1-17

For me, the message written in this book is not just a message, it is a revelation that God gave to me. It comes from my heart. This revelation is something that will absolutely work for you. If you follow its principles, it will change your life in 50 days.

To begin with, I must make clear that I am using the term "debt" very loosely. For me, debt is not just financial, but refers to any negative in your life—anything that you feel is running at a deficit and is leaving you behind. It can mean problems in your marriage for instance. Maybe reading this booklet is your last stop before going to divorce court. Maybe you have problems with your children or other family members.

Maybe you are suffering physically. Your body has a large "debt" it cannot pay. But God can heal you in the name of Christ Jesus!

Perhaps it is an employment problem, or spiritual oppression, or a habit you simply cannot break. And, of course, it may be real financial debt. Whatever problem, whatever mountain, whatever deficit you may have, God can clear it up in the next 50 days.

Why 50 days? The number 50 is an important number in the Bible. It all goes back to the time when the children of Israel came out of Egypt. At the time of their escape, God sent the destroying angel to smite the firstborn of Egypt. But He told Moses to instruct the Israelites, and they slaughtered lambs and put blood on their doorposts and lintels. When the angel saw the blood, he "passed over" their homes, and they did not suffer death. Since that day, when the blood of a lamb saved them, that holy day was called "Passover."

After they escaped, the Israelites traveled through the desert to Mount Sinai. God did miracles during this time (including the deliverance at the Red Sea), but the next important thing in Israel's history was what happened at the Mountain. There, God gave Moses the Ten Commandments and made a covenant with them. The Jews of the first century believed that this happened *50 days* after their forefathers came out of Egypt. The celebration was known as *Pentecost*, because the word means *fifty*.

Pentecost is mentioned in the Old Testament as the Feast of Weeks (Exodus 16:9, Leviticus 23:15, and Numbers 28:26), because it was celebrated *7 weeks* (49 days +1 day) after the Passover. The Feast of Weeks was the time to bring a first fruits offering to the Temple, because it was the main *harvest festival*. It was a time of celebration, rejoicing, and rest.

So, in Jesus' time, Pentecost was a combination celebration—a time to thank God for His covenant, and a time of harvest and enjoying God's abundance.

How does this work, though, in the New Testament? It is really very simple. Jesus died on Good Friday, during the Jewish Passover celebration. As Christians we know that Jesus was our Passover Lamb; it is by His blood that we are saved from death. Yet at the time, His disciples did not understand this. His death through them into great turmoil. They did not understand that He would be raised from the dead. This turmoil parallels all the distress of the Israelites during the final, dark hours before their deliverance. As the disciples said on the road to Emmaus, *"We had hoped He would be the Messiah."* They were so turned around they didn't even realize they were talking to the Master Himself!

But just as light dawned for the Israelites, hope returned to the disciples. Jesus began to appear to them. He appeared to Peter, and to the two on the road, and to the Twelve. He convinced them He was alive. Even doubting Thomas finally believed. According to 1 Corinthians 15, Jesus appeared to over 500 people to convince them He had risen from the dead, and that He was alive.

The question is, did everything turn around for them once they realized Jesus was alive? Was it enough to know that in order to receive the fullness of what God had for them? Surprisingly, the answer is **NO.** God did not choose to do things that way. Instead, Jesus appeared to the Twelve over a period of forty days. During this time, he instructed them. It was a spiritual boot camp—even beyond what they had already experienced with Him for three years.

One day, they were getting impatient with all the waiting. They wanted God to do something big right then. The book of Acts records the conversation: Lord, wilt thou at this time restore again the kingdom to Israel? And he said unto them, It is not for you to know the times or the seasons, which the Father hath put in his own power. But ye shall receive power, after that the Holy Ghost is come upon you: and ye shall be witnesses unto me both in Jerusalem, and in all Judea, and in Samaria, and unto the uttermost part of the earth. Acts 1:6-8 Jesus was saying that God had a plan, and that plan had to do with timing. They would receive miraculous power and deliverance when He had ordained it. That time came to a head after *50 days*, on the Day of Pentecost.

On the Day of Pentecost, God birthed the Church. Unlike Moses, God did not give a Law written on tablets of stone, but a Law written in our hearts. He gave us the law of Christ. Miraculous power was poured out, signs took place, power to preach and witness came, cowards became warriors, and souls were swept into the Kingdom. A new age had dawned. Just like the Feast of Weeks was a harvest festival, now the *spiritual harvest* had come. There was a total 180-degree turnaround in their lives, in their family, in their future... ***in just 50 days!***

In one way, this was a unique, one-time event. We look back and point to it and say, "That's when it happened. The Church was born then. It is history. Our spiritual heritage starts there." But in another way this story gives us spiritual principles. I believe that what happened to the disciples then can happen to us now. There is a spiritual reality in seeking God for 50 days—the time between Passover and Pentecost, the Cross and the Outpouring—and seeing supernatural power as a result. Do you believe God can turn things around in your life in just 50 days?

As I have read this story in God's Word, time and time again, I've noticed some things that these people did. When we see that God's people did something in His word to get results, we shouldn't say, "Wow, that's interesting. Look how they did things way back then." We should imitate them! We should do the same things NOW!

Scripture tells us that God is no respecter of persons. If God will perform miracles for them, God will do it for us, if we meet the same conditions. He will do the same for you when you begin to act upon these seven principles.

Here are seven things the people did to receive their miracle in 50 days.

CHAPTER 2

They Began To Love One Another!

The Bible says in Acts 2:1, *"And they were all with one accord, in one place."*

Before the Day of Pentecost the disciples had competed with one another. They had argued about who was the greatest. They had asked for the best seats in heaven. At the time of Jesus' death, Peter had denied Jesus three times. We know they weren't always in one accord, because Thomas wasn't even there when Jesus appeared to them the first time after His resurrection.

Now all that was gone. They had come together and they were one again. Because they were in one accord, God was able to pour out His Spirit and His miracles upon them.

My point is this: If you do not have love within your heart for your family, if you have unforgiveness, if you are mad at somebody, God cannot bless you. You can try all you can try. You can do all you can do. Your spiritual temperament, like an inner "temperature," has to be right. If it isn't, you'll never reap a harvest. You'll never be able to celebrate the Feast of Pentecost because it is a time of rejoicing over what you've brought in. Others will be dancing, and you'll be empty-handed. Why? Because your insides have to have a good climate to grow a crop. Someone once said, *"You cannot grow tomato plants at the North Pole."*

You cannot have God's miracles and God's blessings if the temperature is cold with unforgiveness, with bruises that have never healed, and hatred towards other people.

The Bible says in Proverbs 10:12, *"Hatred stirreth up strife: but love* covereth all sins."

A woman came to me and said, *"I had an argument with my husband."* That's not why you dislike him. Hatred *causes* the arguments. You can have two people that hate each other, and it doesn't matter what the issue is, they bait each other. People will argue over a ball game, the weather, or anything at all, not because it is worth the fight, but because they have hatred in their life.

But when you love people, it will surpass any difficulty. If you have love in your heart, you can forgive them for anything. But if you have hatred within you, anything will tick you off. Love covers all sin. That is what God wants us to walk in. He wants us to walk in love.

WILLIAM SEYMOUR
LOVE: EVIDENCE OF THE HOLY SPIRIT

William Seymour was the man God used to spark the Azusa Street revival in Los Angeles. Out of this revival, Pentecostal denominations began throughout America and around the world.

Seymour was a black man who preached from an orange crate. He had received the Baptism in the Holy Spirit under Charles Parham's ministry. (It was at Parham's school in Topeka, Kansas that the outpouring of the Spirit was first renewed on January 1, 1901.) Charles Parham had come to Houston, Texas to preach in a local church. Since William Seymour was a black man, he had to sit in the balcony of the church. He was not allowed to sit among the whites in the congregation. Regardless of how *people* treated him, Seymour was filled by *God* with the power of the Spirit.

After the great Azusa Street Revival was in full bloom, Charles Parham came to Los Angeles to witness this move for himself. Upon his arrival in Los Angeles, he was terribly rude and disrespectful to William Seymour because of his color. Seymour was shocked that the man who had ministered the Baptism to him was so filled with prejudice. How could one who spoke in tongues—a gift from God—be so hateful? Because of this, William Seymour wrote in the Azusa Street papers that the main evidence of the Baptism in the Holy Spirit was not speaking in tongues, but was love.

I Corinthians 13:1 says, *"Though I speak with the tongues of men and of angels, and have not love, I become as a sounding brass, and a tinkling symbol."*

It goes on to say, *"Though I bestow all my goods to feed the poor, and though I give my body to be burned, and have not love, it profits me nothing"* (1 Corinthians 13:2-3).

If a person does not operate in love, all of their good works and superficial spirituality is of no value to them.

The Bible says *"Though 1 have faith so that I can re-move mountains, and have not love, 1 am nothing."* This is a remarkable statement. Here the Bible clearly says that faith without love equals **NOTHING.** You cannot be a nothing and have the Baptism of the Holy Spirit. I have known many people who spoke in tongues, but they were critical of everyone and did not have the love of God in them. Even though a person may speak in other tongues, love creates the climate for God to release His breeze of miracles and the supernatural. It makes a way for the harvest God longs for you to have. The most important element of a person being full of God's power is to show the love of God in their life.

This "get-even" attitude—an eye for an eye, and a tooth for a tooth—has to stop. We have to rid our hearts of all re-sentment and walk in the love of God.

God has called every person to walk in love. During the next 50 days, do everything in your power to make things right with those around you. Maybe you need to write a letter to a person or a family member. You need to have your unforgiveness or hatred healed. If you don't get it healed, and you don't begin loving people, God will never be able to get you out of debt. Hatred will rob you of your miracle. So make peace with your enemies. If they don't want to make peace, do what Jesus did and love them anyway. Acting like Jesus opens the way for Jesus to work on your behalf. It opens the way for God to get you out of debt.

CHAPTER 3

They Began To Pray!

There's a lot we don't know about how the early disciples prayed, but there are some details we do know. Among other things, we know that they had a *specific time* to pray. The Bible says in Acts 2:15, ***"These are not drunken as ye suppose, seeing it is but the third hour of the day."*** When it says "third hour" it means 9 AM, because they reckoned the hours of each day starting from 6 AM. The normal times for prayer at the Temple were 9 AM and 3 PM. Why didn't they pray at 6AM? Because they did not have electricity. They waited for the sun to come up and allowed time for people to get there. At 6 AM or at night they could not have seen what to do. So they prayed later.

Things are different for us today. We live in the modern age and can be more productive. We are able to get up and do things. We have to be at work early and keep appointments. The point is not that one time is holier than another, since God is the Creator of all the world. The point is that God honors His people when they set a time and remain faithful to it. In those days, it was 9 AM and 3 PM—the times for community prayer.

When we read the Bible, we see that the most amazing miracles happened at those times:

1. The outpouring on the Day of Pentecost happened at 9 AM (Acts 2:15).

2. Zechariah saw Gabriel at 9 in the morning (Luke 1:10).

3. The lame man was healed by Peter and John at 3 in the afternoon (Acts 3:1).

4. Elijah called fire from heaven at 3 in the afternoon (1 Kings 18:29).

5. Daniel received the revelation from the angel Gabriel at the time of evening prayer (Daniel 9:21).

Why? Does God respect one time more than another? No. These miracles happened when they did because this was the people's set time to pray.

Set a specific time to pray. Stick with that time. As you do, God will meet you in a powerful way. This is the pattern of people that accomplish great exploits for God.

In the time of Daniel, a terrible, profane law had been decreed:

"Whosoever shall ask a petition of any God or man for thirty days, save of thee, O king, he shall be cast into the den of lions"(Daniel 6:7).

What did Daniel do? He went to his home to pray, as was his custom. The Bible says he prayed three times a day: three hours and three times during the day he would go and pray— at 9, 12, and 3 o'clock. He came before God and prayed toward Jerusalem, as was his custom.

They arrested him and threw him in the lion's den. The Bible says in Daniel 6:20, *"But God closed the lion's mouth; and they did him no harm."*

Why? Because he prayed!

Pick a time to pray and stick with that particular time. In the next 50 days, PRAY the same time every day. God will change your situation and circumstances.

A PRAYING PARENT

During the Korean War an American soldier was wounded and pinned down between the North Korean and American lines. The area was known as "Heartbreak Ridge." The officers tried and tried to get someone to attempt a rescue, but the enemy fire was too fierce and no one dared venture into it.

Finally, one soldier looked down at his watch. When the clock showed that the hour had struck, he began to crawl out of the trench. With bullets flying just inches over his head, he reached the wounded man and began to pull him to safety. Once they were back in American lines the lieutenant asked him, "Why did you wait so long to finally save your friend?"

He responded, "I know what time it is back home, and I know when my mother prays every day. Right now my mother is on her knees praying for me!"

We need to have a prayer life that others can set their watch by. If you will go to prayer every day at the same time, God will meet you and miracles will happen.

CHAPTER 4

They Began To Fast!

"These are not drunken as ye suppose, seeing it is but the third hour of the day." Acts 2:15

When the disciples spoke in tongues, people were accusing them of being drunk. To convince them that they had not been drinking, Peter began his argument by saying, *"It is nine o'clock in the morning—it's not possible for us to be drunk!"* The basis for this argument has to do with the Feast of Pentecost. Orthodox Jews fasted on Feast days. They did a half-fast until 3 o'clock in the afternoon. Later in the history of the Church, early Christians copied this practice. Through the fourth and fifth centuries, if communion was to be served, the Church leaders would call for a half-fast, and the people would not eat until 3 o'clock in the afternoon.

When John Wesley discovered this in his studies, he announced to the Methodist Church that no one could be ordained as a Methodist preacher if they did not fast two days a week. These were not prolonged fasts but rather the half-fasts like the early Christians practiced on a weekly basis. This practice of fasting went back to the Orthodox Jews. Peter was simply saying, *"We're Orthodox Jews. This is a Feast Day. This is the Feast of Pentecost. We aren't eating or even drinking water until three o'clock in the afternoon. So we could not be drunk, because we didn't even drink any water."*

His whole argument was that he was fasting for the holy day.

If you want God to turn your situation around, take a day to fast. Set aside the same day every week to fast. If you cannot fast one day for 24 hours, fast two half-days during a week. As you begin to fast God will begin to speak to you and the powers of Satan will be broken off of you in the Name of the Lord.

When you go through the Old Testament and begin to examine the people who fasted, and what happened to them, it's unbelievable to the natural mind.

The three wisest men in the Old Testament were Daniel, Joseph and Solomon. They had many things in common. They were also the wealthiest people. Solomon had the wealth of the world. Daniel was the third wealthiest man in the kingdom of Persia. He greatly prospered under King Darius. In his day, Joseph controlled the wealth of the world.

It should not surprise us that another thing these great men had in common was that they all fasted. Daniel fasted for three years as a young student in a military academy where he was supposed to eat meat that was dedicated to demons. So he refused to eat it and ate vegetables instead. This vegetable fast was a powerful partial fast. At the end of the fasting period, he was ten times wiser than anybody else. When he was 90 years old, Daniel went on a partial fast for 21 days. His life was a life of fasting.

Joseph was thrown into prison because he wouldn't sleep with Potiphar's wife. In those days, people often starved to death when they were in prison. The family had to bring them food for them to survive because the state did not provide food for the prisoners. If someone didn't bring a prisoner any food, they starved to death. Since he was promoted underneath the warden, he found favor with the government; they began to provide him food. Still, it was no "picnic"; Joseph didn't necessarily want to fast all that time, but he was forced to fast.

There was a pattern of fasting. Joseph was a faster.

Although few would recognize it, Solomon was also a mighty man of fasting. He inherited the revelation of fasting from his father David. In fact, Solomon, the richest man ever to walk the earth, was born out of a fast. After David committed adultery with Bathsheba, God judged him by taking the child that resulted from their sin away from them. David fasted for seven days that the child would be spared, but the child died anyway. David's advisers were afraid to tell him the baby had died, fearing he would do something desperate. But when he heard, he got up and ate, explaining, "He cannot come to me, but I will go to him." Some think this fast was a failure. But the Bible says that David went to Bathsheba, and comforted her, and she conceived again. Death was not the result of David's fast—life was! The baby that was born was Solomon, the wisest and richest man ever to live. Fasting brings supernatural prosperity!

David knew and recognized all this, and he taught it to his son. So Solomon grew up in this knowledge. When he dedicated the Temple, God confirmed it to him again. 2 Chronicles 7:14 records the revelation God gave to Solomon: *"If my people, which are called by my name, shall humble themselves, and pray, and seek my face, and turn from their wicked ways; then will I hear from heaven, and will forgive their sin, and will heal their land."*

The Hebrew verb in this verse translated "to humble" indicates a humbling of the flesh through fasting. Solomon wanted his people to realize the power of fasting. He wanted them to prosper, and knew they wouldn't be able to unless they repented *with fasting*.

Through Solomon, God promised to honor His people for fasting. God will honor you for fasting. God will bless you as you take the time to fast.

Though most of our spiritual wisdom comes from the Bible, we can also learn many lessons from other portions of our history. In particular, we can learn from American history and the story of our forefathers. The truth is, the history of America has been a history of prayer and fasting, especially in the first 250 years or so. The interesting thing is that every time the American people fasted, God did miraculous things. Of course, God's response had to do primarily with the spiritual well-being of His people. Fasting led to great revivals and salvation for many. Spiritual oppression was broken over and over. But another benefit of fasting seems to be the prosperity the nation received.

The first recorded example of prosperity through fasting happened in the time of the pilgrims. There was a great drought and all the crops were drying up and dying. The Pilgrim leaders called for a day of fasting and prayer. They fell on their knees and cried out to God. While they prayed and fasted, the Indians who had been friendly with them looked on, and to their amazement storm clouds gathered. A great rain broke, and the crops were saved. The Indians converted to Christianity. Prosperity came as a result of fasting.

Another example happened during the great revival known as the Second Great Awakening. During the 1790s and into the 1800s, great revivals of prayer and fasting broke out all over the country. After a period of spiritual dryness, people turned back to God. There was great spiritual renewal in New England and in the frontier of Ohio and Kentucky.

Yet something else happened just after this revival. In 1803, Napoleon Bonaparte of France made a difficult decision. Overwhelmed with his continual wars with the other European countries, he concluded that he needed cash more than land in North America—land he could hardly defend while he tried to conquer Europe. When President Thomas Jefferson wanted to buy New Orleans from France, Napoleon responded by offering Jefferson all of France's holdings on the North American continent.

This monumental transaction, known as the Louisiana Purchase, was the sale of the century—and one of the greatest real estate deals of all time. On April 30th, 1803 President Thomas Jefferson signed the paperwork and made the purchase for a trifling $15 million. The territory comprised almost 900,000 square miles, or nearly 600 million acres. This averages out to only about four cents an acre for the land that stretches from the Gulf of Mexico to the Canadian border, and eventually became totally or in part the states of Louisiana, Arkansas, Missouri, Iowa, North Dakota, South Dakota, Nebraska, Kansas, Wyoming, Minnesota, Oklahoma, Colorado and Montana. It was impossible then to calculate the wealth contained in this vast land, and it still is today. With the sweep of a pen, America had *doubled!*

Was this coincidence? Well, it seemed to happen again some years later. In the 1840s, under the leadership of Charles Finney, more revival broke out. Finney led thousands to Christ. What's more, Finney was a man devoted to fasting. He wrote:

"I used to spend a great deal of time in prayer; sometimes, I thought, literally praying without ceasing. I also found it very profitable and felt very much inclined to hold frequent days of private fasting."

Finney didn't just fast himself, he taught others to fast. He was the president of Oberlin College in Ohio, and led many into the same life of devotion he practiced. His people fasted and prayed that God would pour out His Spirit, that souls would be saved, and especially that America would repent of the wickedness of slavery.

During this same time, war broke out with Mexico. Armies

first clashed on April 25, 1846, and the war officially ended on February 2, 1848 with the signing of the Treaty of Guadalupe Hidalgo. The end result of this treaty was that America acquired 1.2 million square miles (about 768 million acres) for about 15 cents an acre—another incredible bargain. This land became the states of California, Nevada, Utah, Arizona, New Mexico, and parts of what are now Colorado and Wyoming, as well as the contested land in Texas. America was now more than three times the size it had been 50 years earlier, and now stretched "from sea to shining sea."

This conquest did more than dramatically change the map of the United States. On January 24, 1848 (9 days before the Treaty of Guadalupe Hidalgo that sealed America's acquisition of the land) gold was found at Sutter's Mill in California—land that had belonged to Mexico. News began to leak out about the find, and before long the Gold Rush was on. Prospectors flooded the West, eventually searching for gold throughout the newly conquered territory. The wealth that poured into the U.S. Treasury was staggering. By 1852, California's annual gold production reached a then all-time high of $81 million. During the first five years of the Rush, California produced over $285 million in gold—an amount 21 times greater than the total previous production in the whole of America in these years alone.

In addition to the fabulous quantities of gold found, another great mineral find awaited the nation. Gold-hungry prospectors on their way to California had complained for years of "blasted blue stuff" in western Nevada. They were looking for gold dust, not blue, and moved on, wiping the bluish mud from their boots. In 1859 someone finally decided to analyze the blue stuff. It turned out to be the highest grade silver ore ever found on the North American continent.

The greatest mineral strike in history had been discovered. Known as the Comstock Lode (named after one of the early prospectors in the area), the silver-rich region was soon swamped with miners. From 1859 to 1864 the Comstock Lode yielded over $400 million in silver and gold. Since the dollar in 1860 had a buying power over 21 times that of the dollar today, this is the equivalent of *over $8.5 billion* in modern American dollars. Put in modern terms of our Gross National Product, however, this would be the equivalent of roughly $100 billion. The Comstock Lode hit the United States' economy like a prosperity bomb. In the end, this money financed the Union's military efforts in the Civil War and helped to bring slavery down. This was the very thing Charles Finney fasted and prayed for.

Was all this just coincidence? Judge for yourself. As one man said, ***"When I pray, coincidences happen, when I don't, they don't."*** The same can be said of fasting. Every time America fasted and prayed as a nation, God prospered it incredibly. Why? Fasting brings prosperity, and breaks the chains of debt.

My point is this: If God can turn blue mud into the greatest silver lode ever found; he is big enough to turn your situation around. He wants to prosper you. But fasting is a big part of the process.

In the next *50* days, take one day a week to fast. It will change your life!

CHAPTER 5

They Began Talking Faith

The Bible says that *"sweet and bitter water do not come out of the same fountain"* (James 3:11).You cannot speak healing one minute, speak sickness the next, and expect positive results.

It was Peter that said in Acts 2:16, *"What you're seeing happen, this is that which was spoken by the prophet Joel."* For God to bring about the miracle on the Day of Pentecost, He had to have someone speak it. Joel was chosen hundreds of years before when he prophesied in Joel 2:28, *"And it shall come to pass afterward, that I will pour out my spirit upon all flesh; and your sons and your daughters shall prophesy, your old men shall dream dreams, your young men shall see visions."*

The Bible says that *"death and life are in the power of the tongue"* (Proverbs 18:21). This means that both the good and the bad things that happen to people often are tied up closely with how they speak. This is not superstition, or parroting words you don't mean in order to get a result. It is disciplining your words to line up with your faith. People say *"actions speak louder than words."* Well, for the person of faith, actions *are* words, and words *are* actions. You have to taken action with your tongue if you are going to see faith results.

For instance, you just don't get healed because you show up in "new clothes." You get healed because you started proclaiming it, *"By the stripes of Jesus I am healed!"* And, *"I will not die, but live, and declare the works of the Lord."*

You don't get blessed and financially prosperous just because you are a hard worker. There are a lot of hard workers in the world. You can go to Third World countries all over the globe—India, Haiti, and many places in South America and Africa—and see many hard working people. Contrary to what many people say, poor people in these places work very hard to survive, yet most remain impoverished and even starve to death.

Why? As hard as it is for us to understand, God is a God of faith. He is full of compassion, but He responds to faith. It is **FAITH** that is *"the substance of things hoped for"*—not just need. You get blessed because you harness your tongue and make it obey the Word of God. You begin to speak God's promises, *"God is blessing me. God is opening up the windows of heaven. God has given to me new opportunities."* It takes faith.

Now, someone may say, *"I am going to try it... 'I am prosperous. I'm prosperous. I'm saying it by faith.' You know, it's a hard thing to say because I don't have the money, but I'm prosperous!"*

Friend, if your confessions of faith flow out of two sides of your mouth, you are not going to prosper. As I said, it has to be real—you can't just be a parrot. The words you confess have to be a part of you. You have to meditate on the Word and get a revelation—even if it's only the size of a mustard seed—and take it from there. As you speak the promises of God and make all your confession and conversation agree with these promises, God will bless you. You must have this attitude, *"I believe it with all of my heart, God is beginning to do it in the Name of the Lord."*

THE SHUNAMMITE WOMAN

Do you remember the story of Elisha? A Shunammite woman, who knew he was a great prophet of God, built an extra room for him on her house. He stayed there when he came through their area of the country. Elisha was so grateful he wanted to do something for her. He found out she was wealthy, but couldn't have children. A son would be the greatest gift.

When Elisha told her that she would have a son, her faith was weak. *"Oh, no,"* she said, *"Don't get my hopes up and break my heart."* But Elisha had faith for her, and his confession prevailed. He prayed and prophesied; and she had a son.

The years passed and the baby grew to be a boy. One day while working in the fields with his father, the boy fell sick. His father took him home, but it was too late; that day he died. The woman laid him on the bed, then told her servants, *"Saddle up the old donkey there, and don't slow down unless I tell you to. We are going to find Elisha."* She got on that donkey. If it were today, she would be driving 100 miles an hour. She began to look for the prophet of God. Some person asked them, *"What's the trouble, why are you going so fast?"*

The book of 2 Kings tells us that her response to everyone who asked her why she was going to Elisha in such a hurry was simply, *"All is well."* When Elisha saw her coming, he sent his servant Gehazi to see what was wrong. *What's the trouble?"* he asked. She said, *"All is well. Show me Elisha!"* Well, the fact was that all was **NOT** well. Her heart was broken. Her son was dead, lying in the bed that Elisha stayed in. But her confession was, *"All is well."*

What made her say something like that?

Her faith in God. She remembered how Elisha's prophecy was a word of faith, and she was putting that lesson into practice. The same faith that gave the boy life the first time would save him now. Elisha went and raised the boy from the dead and gave him back to his mother. At that point, all *was* well. The facts fell in line with her faith. That's the way it needs to be with us today. We need to see that facts serve faith, not the other way around. We enforce this truth through our confession.

Faith can move mountains. It can cause the devil to get off your back and take his hand off your bank account. It can cause the devil's power to be broken off your boss so you can find favor with him. It can get you promoted. It opens up the doors of blessing upon you.

But it takes faith, in the Name of Jesus. Like the Shunammite, we have to declare, **"IT IS WELL!"**

By the way, there are no "buts." That is the vocabulary of those that have been defeated by the devil. It is the vocabulary of doubt and unbelief. It's the vocabulary of those that make an excuse. They always end up blaming God, *"Oh, it can't be me. I'm so wonderful and so blessed and intelligent and so smart and so educated and so religious. It can't be my problem, it's God's problem. And God just doesn't want me to be blessed. That's the kind of person He is."*

Friend, there is no badness in God, just like there is no goodness in the devil. The Bible tells us very pointedly: *"__Do not err__, my beloved brethren. Every good gift and every perfect gift is from above, and cometh down from the Father of lights, with whom is no variableness, neither shadow of turning"* (James 1:16-17). What is James saying? He is saying, "Watch out! Don't let the devil trick you! If it's good, it's from God. If it's bad, it's from the devil. It's that simple." This means that if all the pistons aren't firing, the trouble is on our end, or the devil is attacking us. You just need to get your mind and priorities straightened out.

CHAPTER 6

They Believed God For Their Finances

"And my God shall supply all your need according to His riches in glory by Christ Jesus."—Philippians 4:19

When Jesus was crucified on the cross, the disciples felt hopelessness and despair. Even though we might not think about it, part of their distress was financial. Since people supported their work, Jesus' ministry provided for their financial needs. Their "paycheck" covered the expenses of the household. Now, with Jesus gone, it seemed they were without money.

In John 21:3, Peter said, *"I go a fishing."*

The reason Peter was going fishing is because that had been his vocation. This is how he made a living. If he had been a carpenter, he would have said, "I'm going to go build a house." If he had been in the real estate business, he would have listed a piece of property. But he was a fisherman.

"Simon Peter saith unto them, I go a fishing. They say unto him, We also go with thee. They went forth, and entered into a ship immediately; and that night they caught nothing. But when the morning was now come, Jesus stood on the shore: but the disciples knew not that it was Jesus. Then Jesus saith unto them, Children, have ye any meat? They answered him, No. And he said unto them, Cast the net on the right side of the ship, and ye shall find. They cast

therefore, and now they were not able to draw it for the multitude of fishes."—John 21:3-6

The scripture goes on to describe the catch. It was a "multitude of fishes," "great fishes," "a hundred and fifty-three" fish in total number.

If I were to go fishing, I would take a fishing rod and some worms. However, Peter used a boat and fishing nets. He did this because he was a commercial fisherman—he wasn't fishing for fun. He believed to catch fish so he could sell them on the market and pay his bills.

Yet there is a deeper truth here. Peter wasn't just going fishing because he had bills to pay. Peter was discouraged. He had denied the Lord. He doubted his call to the ministry. The fact that he was out of money only made this worse. When Jesus appeared to the disciples and gave them the great catch of fishes, He was providing right then and he was making a promise for the future. Jesus was saying, ***"Don't be discouraged. I am the Provider. I will provide for you, and you won't have to worry about money as you minister. Reach the world with the Gospel. Feed my Lambs."***

That's the way it is for us today. This money thing isn't all about you. It is about reaching the world. It is true that God counts the sincerity of every offering according to what a person has and can give. But it is also true that it takes a lot of money to spread the Gospel. If you are deep in debt, it is harder to give to ministries that are reaching the world. God wants to get the money issue out of the way in your life so you can give. As 2 Corinthians 9:11 (NIV) says, ***"You will be made rich in every way so that you can be generous on every occasion."*** God wants to prosper you in the next 50 days, and wants to set you on a path for permanent blessing. Claim that God has "multitude" of blessings, "great blessings," one hundred fold blessings for you!

During this 50-day period, pray that God would open up the windows of heaven and He will pour you out a blessing that you have never received before. This is the time for an avalanche of money to come into your life:

1. For blessings to come upon you...
2. For inheritances to come your way...
3. For new business to come knocking on your door...
4. For you to get promoted...
5. For your children to get college scholarships...

There is no end to what God can do! But you must believe God for your finances!

BIBLICAL PROSPERITY BEGINS IN PRAYER

You remember the story of Jeremiah. Some of the people who listened to his prophecies included Daniel, Shadrach, Mishach, Abednego, and Ezekiel; they all lived in that same time period and listened to Jeremiah's teaching.

When the Babylonians conquered Jerusalem, it was a time of great distress and pain for the people of Judah. Many doubted God and felt He had abandoned them. They were carted off in captivity to Babylon.

While many were off in Babylon, Jeremiah was still in Jerusalem. He wrote a powerful letter to the exiles and sent them an incredible message. When they were saying, *"We are prisoners. There's no hope for us now. What can God do for us here?"*—in that situation Jeremiah challenged them to prosper. He wrote, *"Seek the peace and prosperity of the city to which I have carried you into exile. Pray to the LORD for it, because if it prospers, you too will prosper"* (Jeremiah 29:7, NIV).

We can just imagine how they received this letter. Put yourself in their shoes. How can we pray for prosperity here?

Psalm 137 says they couldn't even sing there—how could they pray that God would bless Babylon? Yet they chose to believe God's word. So they **PRAYED**, just like Jeremiah told them to. And prayers prospered them where they were. It turned lemons into lemonade.

Soon, the Babylonians saw the favor of God upon them. They promoted them and blessed them. Put in today's terms, those little slaves started out cleaning the tables, but they ended up owning the restaurant!

That is what God will do for you!

So the years passed. The Persians had conquered the Babylonians, but many of the Jews were still in bondage. Now, Nehemiah and Ezra had been raised up. They wanted to go back home. They said, "We're going back to our land. We need money to take back. We need gold. We need silver."

The offerings began to come in. In today's money it would be millions and millions of dollars. God blessed the Jews. They became like the Cedars of Lebanon. They became like the palm trees in the middle of the desert. They blossomed, and they prospered.

> *The righteous shall flourish like the palm tree: he shall grow like a cedar in Lebanon.*
>
> *Those that be planted in the house of the LORD shall flourish in the courts of our God.*
>
> *They shall still bring forth fruit in old age; they shall be fat and flourishing;*
>
> *To show that the LORD is upright: he is my rock,*
>
> *and there is no unrighteousness in him.*
>
> *- Psalm 92:12-15*

Why?

Because they prayed that way!

Maybe you are not praying the right prayers. Start praying, *"God, thank you for your blessings. Thank you for meeting my needs. Thank you that I have more than enough. I am the head, and not the tail. I am not going broke. I am going over in Jesus' name. Father, you are meeting me in an abundant manner— in Jesus' Name."*

We don't serve a cheap God who can barely make it and says, *"I can't answer that prayer this month. You have more bills than I can handle. You are going to have to do this on your own."*

God is the God of abundance that will open the windows of heaven and pour out a blessing that you cannot even contain. So you plant a seed. You change the way you pray. You believe God; and God opens the windows of heaven for YOU... in the next 50 days!

CHAPTER 7

They Were All Filled With The Holy Ghost

"They were all filled with the Holy Ghost and began to speak in other tongues as the Spirit gave them utterance."— Acts 2:4

God filled all the disciples with the Holy Ghost. Whatever you do, don't try to do this without the Holy Ghost. It's the Holy Ghost that gives the impartation of power. It is the Holy Spirit that touches you and enables you to rise up and outrun the king's horses as Elijah did. It's the Holy Spirit that gives you the ideas.

There are a lot of people that think they can accomplish a lot of things because of their education, because of their talents, or because of some other thing about themselves. That road has a dead end.

You need the Holy Spirit. The Bible says He sent the Comforter to be alongside of you to help: to help you in YOUR life! He's not there just to help you with some spiritual idea, but to help you to get your work done. He wants to help in everything. If it's worth doing, it's worth asking the Spirit to help. He is by your side even to help you in your business.

The Holy Spirit came to help you deal with your family. He wants to help you to live a life here on this earth. God has called us to be kings and priests and reign with him. Begin to pray in the Spirit every day, especially in the next 50 days!

FOUR THINGS HAPPEN WHEN ONE RECEIVES THE BAPTISM OF THE HOLY SPIRIT

There are FOUR things that take place when you receive the Baptism in the Holy Spirit:

1. **You receive power to be witnesses for Christ.** Acts 1:8 says, *"But ye shall receive power after that the Holy Ghost has come upon you, and ye shall be witnesses."* There is a boldness to speak to others about Christ as you have never done before.

2. **There is an impartation of the power of Jesus into your life.** In John 14: 12, Jesus told the disciples about what would happen after the Baptism of the Holy Spirit took place. *"I say to you, he who believes in Me, the works that I do he will do also; and greater works than these will he do."*

The same miracles Jesus did He wants us to do through Him. He wants you to heal the sick, cast out devils, and release miracles. That empowerment comes through the Baptism of the Holy Spirit.

3. **The Holy Spirit anoints your vocal cords.** Acts 2:4 says, *"They spake in other tongues as the Spirit gave the utterance."* Why? Every miracle God ever performed in creation, every miracle Jesus performed was spoken into existence.

We human beings are the only beings in God's creation that can speak. This is part of the reason the Bible says we are created in the image of God. In the same way, we are to speak the things of God. Now through the Baptism of the Holy Spirit we can speak a language spoken in heaven. It is a creative language. No one has ever been cursed, criticized or defamed in this language. It is a power language of the Spirit. It is speaking and praying the perfect will of God.

> **4. You can use that prayer language anytime you want to**. Paul said in I Corinthians 14:13, *"I will pray in the spirit. I will pray with my understanding also."* Notice it comes from the "will." Jude 20 says, *"Building up your most holy faith, praying in the Holy Ghost."* Every time you pray in tongues, your spirit man gets stronger.

To many people "tongues" is a great hurdle in their spiritual walk. Some have been taught against it and it is difficult for some to receive. If you have not received the Baptism in the Spirit, I recommend you simply ask Jesus to fill you. Then worship the Lord in your own language. After a while get quiet and listen to your "spirit man." Words will begin to rise from your solar plexus area. Jesus said, *"Out of your belly shall flow rivers of living water. But this He spake concerning the Holy Spirit, whom those believing in Him would receive"* (John 7:38-39).

Begin to speak those spirit words and you will begin to release a river of the Holy Ghost.

I know a man named Gene who had a powerful experience with the Holy Spirit. Gene was a man who had many struggles in his life. Temptations and addictions had plagued him for years. While on a fast we were prayer walking in our city. I prayed for him to receive the Baptism of the Holy Spirit. He began to speak the "spirit words." It made all the difference in his life. He became a man incredibly on fire for God. It will make all the difference in your life, too.

Every time you are praying in the Holy Ghost, you are praying in the will of God (Romans 8:27) and building up your faith. You get "faith muscles." Flex your muscles a little bit! Trust the Holy Spirit.

Talk with the Holy Ghost, *"Show me, Holy Spirit, what we are going to do today. God, show me what to do."* If you'll open up to the Spirit, He can turn your life around. He did it for the early believers in just 50 days!

CHAPTER 8

Expect A Miracle

"Give, and it shall be given unto you; good measure, pressed down, and shaken together, and running over, shall men give into your bosom. For with the same measure that ye mete withal it shall be measured to you again."—Luke 6:38

When the apostles came to the upper room on the Day of Pentecost, they were *expecting* God to do something. They did not come just thinking this was another festival day on the Jewish calendar. It was not "business as usual." The final ten days of the fifty day period was one of intense prayer. They surrounded themselves with people of faith. They focused their faith. It was a time that God was going to move. They believed that something powerful was going to take place.

For miracles to happen in your life, you must believe for them. You must believe that something powerful is about to happen in your life.

When I am believing God for something to happen, I've found that I need to do something on my part. If I want to have the lights on, I need to flip the switch. If the car is to start, I must turn the key. If you are going to receive from God, you must learn to always plant a seed.

Seed faith is one of the most powerful laws on the face of the earth. The Bible says in Genesis 8:22, *"As long as the earth remaineth, there is seed time and harvest."* What happens in the natural realm when we plant a seed also happens in the unseen realm when we plant an offering and aim it for spiritual reasons.

The principles of seed faith are as follows:

1. **God is our source.** Your job is not your source. The government is not your source. They may be avenues through which God supplies your need, but ultimately God is your source. If your job were your source, and it went out of business, then your ability to ever achieve anything has dried up with it. But when God is your source, you have an eternal spring of blessing. God reigns forever and He will always supply your needs.

2. **You must plant a seed.** You must aim your seed at a target like you would aim an arrow at the bull's eye. You must believe God specifically as you give your offerings. Believe God for healing. Believe God for your marriage. Believe God for a better job. This is not buying God's blessing, because God's blessings are free. They are too expensive to buy. Rather, it is making a concrete expression of your faith. This is biblical. You will see God multiply back to you exactly in the same manner as you planted.

3. **Expect a miracle**. I've heard people say, "Well, I give, but I don't expect God to give back to me." That sounds spiritual, but really it's not. I never met a farmer who planted a crop that did not expect to have a harvest. I've never seen a gardener plant tomatoes, and not expect tomatoes to come up. When you give to God, expect God to meet you and bless you. This is His will. No earthly father wants to hear their child say, *"Yeah, old dad is a nice guy and means well, but I don't really expect anything out of him. He is never going to do anything for me."* What father would

consider such a statement a courtesy? In the same way, it is hurtful to our heavenly father to know we don't really depend on Him or expect Him to bless us. The fact is, God *delights* in our dependence on Him and *wants* us to expect a blessing.

If you will plant in faith, your personal Day of Pentecost— the *harvest festival*—will come true for you. It will come to pass in God's timing.

There was a lady who was driving in Kansas. She ran out of gas. She was about 50 miles from the nearest service station when a gas truck pulled up behind her. She asked if the driver would give her a ride to the next city. He said, *"Ma'am, I can do that. But I've got the gas to deliver at the next city. Why don't I give you some gas from here?"* He didn't need to give her a ride—he was the source for the service station she was trying to get to!

The same is true of us. We don't need the service station—we have the source! God wants us to plant seeds and expect a miracle. Seed faith turns on the switch.

You must believe your miracle is going to happen. *"Hope deferred maketh the heart sick: but when the desire cometh, it is a tree of life"* (Proverbs 13:12).

This message came from the very throne of God. God said to me, *"All you are doing is delivering mail."*

I'm just a postman. I'm just delivering a "letter" (these words of blessing and encouragement) to you. But YOU are going to have to sign for it. It is "certified." It's got your name on it. If you don't sign for it, you don't receive it. You've got to sign for it in faith. You've got to believe God for it.

You must expect a miracle!

Over the years, there have been people that have come to

my church. There have been rich, poor, educated, unlearned, white, black, and hundreds of families from the international community. I've seen how God has blessed them. I know that God is a blesser.

There was a man who came to our church. We trusted God that he would get a job, and he got a job working for a coal company. He was soon promoted. Finally, he was elevated to the post of professional economist.

I never called him that, but that's what the president called him when they used his estimations for the White House!

God said that you would stand before the mighty. He said *"Be thou diligent in thy business, thou shalt stand before kings."* In this case, God raised the brother up and they called him to the White House to be an adviser to the president.

There was a man in our church who sold cars. He was going through a difficult time and couldn't even make his house payment. He said, "Would you please pray for me? I need to make my house payment." At the time, I could hardly make mine either. But I had about $350 and I said, *"Here, I want to give this to you!"*

Did you know what happened to him? God began to bless him. Now he has two car lots. He has given to this church over the years—one year he gave the church over $10,000! What happened? God blessed him and God promoted him.

Billy Boren was a man that came to this church with an eighth grade education. He could hardly read. He met and married a cultured and beautiful young lady in the church. Her family totally opposed the marriage because they felt she was marrying below herself.

One Sunday he came to church and got saved. Then God called him to preach. At the time, Billy was hanging drywall for a living. It is tough work that wears a man out. He went to

Bridgeport, Texas, and began to pastor a little church. On the side he hung drywall to support his family.

While there, God began to bless him. He made a little money off a project, so he put some money on a little rental piece of property. Then he bought another rental, and then another. He became the wealthiest person in Bridgeport, Texas—and he was still pastoring this little church!

Finally, he called his brother to pastor the church. Then he received a call from his superintendent who said, *"There's this little, small church in McGregor, Texas, down by Waco. I want you to go down there and build a church."*

Billy drove to McGregor. There were only 12 people in the church. He said, *"God's called me here to build a church. God's put it into my heart what we are going to do. We are going to build a big sanctuary, school, gymnasium We're claiming this town for God!"*

That next Saturday he went to get a haircut. There was one of the church deacons in the barbershop. He didn't know Billy was the new pastor. He said, *"Yep. We've got a new pastor coming up here He is going to come in tomorrow and is going to preach. We're going to run him out of town!*

So Billy went to church the next day, not knowing what to expect. As he got up to preach, and this old deacon who had cut his hair stood up. He said, *"Brother Boren, my neck hurts, will you pray for my neck?"*

Brother Boren said, *"Yes, I'll pray for your neck,"* and he laid hands on him. He prayed like he had never prayed before. God healed the deacon's neck! Of course, Billy found favor with him and the whole church.

Things began to explode there in McGregor, Texas. In the end, they built a big church, a gymnasium, and a school. God blessed them mightily.

In the next *50* days, God will **<u>BLESS</u>** you!

God can open the windows of heaven for you.

You may say, *"Well, Brother Bob, I don't have any talents at all. What can I do?"*

Can you dig for fishing worms? I knew a fellow who did exactly that! He caught and sold fishing worms. He was an alcoholic, but I had given his mother a Bible. When she died she passed it on to him. He ended up coming to church and accepting Christ. At the time, we were in one of our worst winters.

He told me, *"Brother Bob, I am going to be broke. All my worms are going to die!"* I went over to his house and prayed for his worms. When the thaw came, he said, *"You won't believe it, but even after that cold, I have more worms than you can believe. I've never seen so many worms!"*

He made a fortune in worms!

My point is you can make a fortune in **anything** if you will trust God!!

God can **DO ANYTHING** for you. Right now—-and every day in the next *50* days-——expect God to perform a miracle over your life!

Do you need a miracle in the next *50* days?

Do you need to get out of debt in the next *50* days?

Remember this...

None of this will work if you are unfaithful to your spouse, if you've got a stack of pornography, if you are getting drunk, lying, cheating, are mean to your wife and children, or not honest at work. God will **<u>NOT</u>** bless you!

You've got to love people.

The Bible says, ***"Don't let the sun go down on your wrath."*** If you hold a grudge, it is a sin. If you go to bed mad, it becomes a sin.

But if you clean out your heart, get right, and put into practice the spiritual principles from the Word of God that I've discussed in this book, God will bless you. He'll get you out of that hole you're in, and make you the head and not the tail.

Trust the Lord and claim His word. He says,

"The LORD shall open unto thee his good treasure, the heaven to give the rain unto thy land in his season, and to bless all the work of thine hand: and thou shalt lend unto many nations, and thou shalt not borrow. And the LORD shall make thee the head, and not the tail; and thou shalt be above only, and thou shalt not be beneath; if that thou hearken unto the commandments of the LORD thy God, which I command thee this day, to observe and to do them" — *Deuteronomy 28:12-13*

This promise is for you, if you will rise up and claim it.

Let me pray the prayer of faith for you right now:

"Lord Jesus, take out of me any sin, any hard feelings, anything that would hinder my prayers from being answered. Lord, You did it for the Early Church. In 50 days, You gave them direction, blessings, healings, and miracles. Lord, You can do it for me. I want to serve You without sin, without malice, and without envy. Forgive me Lord Jesus, with the Blood of Christ. Father, may faith be in my heart. May I always pray. May I continually seek You; and may You speak to me. Open the windows of heaven. Show me what to do. Give direction in my life. Help me to get out of debt. Help me to make it financially. Help my children to be blessed May they draw closer to You. May my body be healed. May my marriage be strong. May nothing be impossible, oh God! Father, I depend upon you. You are the source of my life. Amen."

In the next 50 days, do what the Early Church believers did to receive their miracles:

1. LOVE
2. PRAY
3. FAST
4. TALK FAITH
5. BELIEVE FOR FINANCES
6. BE FILLED WITH THE HOLY SPIRIT
7. EXPECT A MIRACLE!

Begin to praise the Lord. Constantly look to the Father. We are a needy people. We cannot make it without Him.

Write down on a piece of paper what you are believing to receive from God.

I want you to guard every word you say. Speak with confidence and with boldness, and with a prophetic word.

God will deliver you. God will help you. God will show you what to do. Nothing will be impossible in the Name of Jesus.

I rebuke the curse of poverty. Maybe you've been bound by a habit. I rebuke the habits the devil has put upon you. I come against violence, tempers, and anger.

You can achieve greatness in the Name of the Lord. Creativity will come upon you. May God give you new ideas and show you what to do. May you hear God's voice! May the Spirit of God come upon your life!

Speak faith in the Name of the Lord!

By faith, speak what it is going to be like in *50* days! Speak to your money, your family, and your situation.

Proclaim God's blessings! With God, NOTHING IS IMPOSSIBLE!

I want to know how God got you out of debt in *50* days!
If this book has been a blessing to you, feel free
to contact me at:

BOB RODGERS MINISTRIES

6900 Billtown Road

Louisville, KY 40299

Bobrodgersministries.org

TEN THINGS I WILL DO IN THE NEXT 50 DAYS TO GET OUT OF DEBT!.

1. _____

2. _____

3. _____

4. _____

5. _____

6. _____

7. _____

8. _____

9. _____

10. _____

Visit Pastor Bob Rodgers on the
Internet:

www.worldprayercenter.org
www.prayerradio.net

Fasting and Prayer Books
By Dr. Bob Rodgers

21 Days That Will Revolutinize Your Life
Price: $10.00

Patterns Of Prayer That Will Change Your L:ife!
Price: $6.00

Jesus Taught His Disciples To Pray For Every Need Of Life
Price: $10.00

BOB RODGERS MINISTRIES

6900 Billtown Road

Louisville, KY 40299

Bobrodgersministries.org